# Excontemporary

# Excontemporary

poems

# Beth Baruch Joselow

Story Line Press | *Pasadena, CA*

*Excontemporary*

Grateful acknowledgement is made to the following magazines, which have
published some of these poems: *Shiny*, *Texture*, *lower limit speech*, and *Exposures*.

ISBN 978-1-58654-101-9 (tradepaper)
      978-1-58654-102-6 (casebound)

The National Endowment for the Arts, the Los Angeles County Arts Commission, the
Ahmanson Foundation, the Dwight Stuart Youth Fund, the Max Factor Family Foun-
dation, the Pasadena Tournament of Roses Foundation, the Pasadena Arts & Culture
Commission and the City of Pasadena Cultural Affairs Division, the City of Los Ange-
les Department of Cultural Affairs, the Audrey & Sydney Irmas Charitable Foundation,
the Kinder Morgan Foundation, the Meta & George Rosenberg Foundation, the Aller-
gan Foundation, the Riordan Foundation, Amazon Literary Partnership, and the Mara
W. Breech Foundation partially support Red Hen Press.

Second Edition
Published by Story Line Press
an imprint of Red Hen Press
www.redhen.org

*For Thea, Ethan and Gabe Joselow, always*

# Contents

# Excontemporary

# Blacker Pacific

Travel this glass canyon
on your back, on a sled
pulled by dogs blue with fear.

As long as the blankets
are thick, and the medicine
takes, you may arrive at base

without having lost it all.
Don't tumble or drag
a finger through the snow.

Even the smallest arch
is a figure of strength, bending
its back to hold the load. That

scratch of the runner on glass can't
come to seem musical, but with luck
it can be polished out

until what is reflected,
clear as a bell, is the journey
itself, the tale you'll tell.

# Bed Window Door

Hands put together

    in tandem in a sharp

bark like laughing not

to forget a dark

    family framed by a barred

window or door, a barbed

    bed put together in the dark

door behind a sharp

    bark like laughing in tandem

like two put together to forget

    a sharp bed framed

by barbed laughing behind

    the family window or door

a barred family barks

    to forget family together

like two barks or barbs

hands in tandem put

together sharp like laughing.

## Absence of Assurance

The carrots had been moved
to another aisle.
It was unexpectedly cold
in those long lines listing
to the left.
        Fear, then later
camps and conflict, called for
extreme prudence, virtue
in people like ourselves.

The sigh meant
the sphere of daily life,
listening attentively
for a hoarse calling out
in French on a
West German program.

Professions for Jews
remain a problem:
*"You are right. It
would be the way."*
Few recordings exist
of those unbelieving
buildings and neighborhoods.

Is somber concern
a crowning achievement,
is it true, her early years
all spent? What comes after
she stuck her neck out?
More bread? When?
On this aisle?

# Narcissus

Elected, I become the prince
and dream in this tuck in the seams.

Your disparagement is weightless
as I invent the parachute

to drift above the earth
passing judgment. Oh

wait a minute, oh won't
you please tuck me in, Mom?

Transformed, unhindered,
a wish to sleep dominated by

the primal need for an object,
I tell you I need nothing.

A sensual and variable
ball about three feet in diameter,

so it is held, so well may be.
You will find it refreshing

up there, balanced between
your arches; you are flat

in the day's residues (you
know what they are called).

Happy circumstance! An excitable
ego, pleased with each

of its organs! I know
I have your attention now.

But you want to talk about sleep
while I want to close my eyes

neglecting the investigations
forced upon us by our discovery.

# Love

He mixes love up with the girl. He thinks of the abstract
but he sees a representational figure and he uses her to fill
in all the blanks. It's something he learned. But she's so
blank the fill-ins look white, and it ends up white on
white, no page you can see without thinking about art, and
he doesn't want to bring art into this. Maybe he doesn't
but it's there all the same and now it's got to be dealt with.
Meanwhile, the girl keeps getting bigger, in fact, she
wasn't a girl at all, not for years. She does not have love on
her mind, although it feels like it's infused throughout her
body and works there something like magnesium, which
she's heard you can't do without. So actually, she probably
has a significant amount of love on her mind, a measurable
amount anyway. Why she has to be so elliptical I'll never
know. Typical of her kind. The art part is getting dis-
gusted. This narrative remains on the emotional plane so
far and art doesn't want to be kept there, even if it admits
to similar origins. Let's talk theory. Okay, but theory's not
my strong suit. Theoretically, he loves the girl, but really,
she's not a girl at all, so where does that leave us? Aren't
you tired of these love stories that aren't love stories at all
but just another dodge?

# Old Soul

A prolonged period of
        living in the ether of gossip
its resultant erudition
        an unsought consequence.
The soul unravels from the body
        wishing to identify
and name itself anew.

Why would this soul
        in the storyteller's grasp
be imagined as birdlike
        when with the passage of time
the soul grows heavier as
        it carries the weight
of the body.

An old soul pushing a barrow
        of loosened ideas,
an old frame in which
        all of the joints squeak.

This is the burden to put down
        in quiet celebration
appropriate music crooned
        by a single instrument,
        a solitary voice,
working in unison.

# Sometimes Orchid

Clogged by memories jogged
at the party, running out to run up

big bills as an antidote to folly.
She should not expect

to be all happy. He likes
African music, comes from Chicago but

it is not the same.
The exchange is similar to the one for

Forest Park, but it stands for
Mineral, or sometimes Orchid.

The party line is busy with
unexpressed information

burning like bricks containing
an actual fire.

Similarly with me I said
"*Same here,*" and passed up

another round, having been thought
to say, "*Put 'er there.*"

My hand in the pocket
of the Secretary of War,

for an instant we entered a phase
of denial while the fire

made things hard inside.
Everything came rushing up,

spilling back in the kind
of zealous spilling that is  often

the counterpart of a good time.

# Pair of Glasses

Make a frame for it
A comfort, a construct.

Show promise and adaptability
Get on with it,

Plan, devise, contrive
A rule that brings order

To our perceptions
Although specific problems

Persist, even if
Not now framed

In the poignancy of the hero's failure.
That ubiquitous figure,

A figure out of clay,
The sorrowing mother.

Draft a man to fit or adjust
To an end. Regulate, arrange

My face to all occasions.
Teach the student what children are like.

Required to pass tests, order
And disorder. Room for ruin

To form the mouth and lips
To form soundlessly

*"We're pleased to see you"*
Running in to cool and then solidify.

No particular outcome is assured.
The horizontal frame line

Does not appear on the screen.
Stay anyway.

# Happenstance

Back in the railroad flat one of us was dancing and one of us was hammering at the walls to keep the trains at bay. That fence wasn't worth a plugged nickel and the dance required proper shoes but the music went right on and the shuffle began all over again. They came to the back of the room with their hands out and looked longingly at the larder. What could there have been to report, how forestall their pangs in the night. It was a crackerbarrel kind of justice so we just strung them up and rewound the Victrola. Light was just beginning to break around the corner where you could just about make out its hot glow. But that was a long time ago and this time when I took you to dinner and a show none of it mattered anymore. We took off our shoes in the dark and stretched our toes long and apart and no one could see, no one knew.

# In Your Image

Exactly like
The response I would have made

To subsequent experience,
A basic attitude

Like the use of sleep
For death

Or anyone else, such as
A figure of speech

What would I have done
For focus, treasuring an amulet

A holy system sculpted
Of gauze in a dream

Of need. Humiliation
Turned in a vivid manner

To a native landscape
Stippled with

Outsized animals
So gentle that

Loss is in retreat
On a straight path

From object to ideal,
From sacred to human.

## Accept the Practice

Having determined a time frame,
the possibilities lodged in it,
the fractures likely to occur

she was able to extricate
the ball from the net this time
and return to the server's position.

No fault. No fault line. The step
hesitant at first struck ground,
steadied her in warrior pose

then reverse triangle, then leaning
into the wind, lofting the ball
without intervention or instrument.

Wasn't it a wow, being invisible,
crowdless, crowing,
dissonant but honest, glad of it.

## On One's Mettle

Challenged or aroused
  by an honest gunman

For the spirited drama
  the performance of a wildcat

Her blend of nervous fancy
  temper finer than prose

In relation to a given situation
  not always easy to see

Poetry might be
  but never apparently dreamed

This disposition gets it
  over the wall

Trucks it from town to town
  until a light goes on

The boundary district enlarges
  with impromptu characterizations

Nothing gets told
  just the same way

Having used in combination
  spirit, ardor, courage and stamina,

Staying up all night
  with a purpose.

## Money Box

It's a box this money business, no question, but control the
world, fox the foxy, come out with both hands raised in
front of your face. Imagine the circumstances for winning a
friend of the boss, the big cheese. We heard he makes one
million eight annually. Before taxes. In Paris. It's still
raining; ships collide on the sea. Well, almost easier to do
without on a vegetable farm in a likeable climate growing
maryjane among the rutabagas, rustling the tent flaps with
the barrel of a rifle. Perfect your attitude, hitchhike your
way to the diligent gardener's. He'll have something you
can do for your next meal.

Meanwhile, back in New York City, even Tokyo, they
haven't given you a second thought. You don't wear scents
and they can't compute the insensible. There's a formula
not only for success that is said to be a secret formula, but
we know better. Punch drunk Cathedral dwellers walk off
the end of the dock. Out front another car blows up with-
out a blink from passersby. If the money's not in oil any-
more what has it gone to? We know a lot of pockets are
remaining empty, you can figure on some residual power in
uselessness, but it's not so much compared to the array of
divertissements at FAO Schwarz. You can find it from the
firetower. Look out. Lick that spoon. Give it a swipe with
your handkerchief. Don't pretend to toss it away, pretend
to start over.

Everyone invents a box to put money in, a way to fit the
money into the box then have the box make money by
itself; that way if the world sits on its hands, nothing has to
stand still.

## What Is Owed

No one can touch this
Feeble architecture of marked bills.

Repayment sits in the wings
In the interstices

Waiting for a line.
Relish the thought

A palm rubbed the wrong way
Dips into its blisters

Settles for a summary statement
Barters for a little grace

This is only gravy
This is only messenger service

If they are late
You don't have to pay them.

## To Get Alternative

I want to go back to air,
Pre-sound, backtrack
Prior to words, what's been

Shared, this tube,
I said:
Don't fence me in.

Recombinant, crossing over
Into union, uncalled for
Characters in definition

When time called for
No definition but radical
Eradication, free

For the first
Time, a particle in space,
Practically unknown,

Apart in the uncharted
Parts. Let's keep it
That way. Name

The territory and it becomes
*The Louisiana Purchase*,
Advantage lost

To *Sea of Nectar*,
*Amazonis, Ambrosia,*
*Antigones Fons.*

No *Delilah*, no place
Left to author
Some other history.

*

Let's live
At the window a while,
Adjusting the blinds.

# Tentative History

An imagined line
relating to a hellbent hour

of too much visible
activity. What went wrong?

The particulars synthesized
but were never painted.

Women embracing farm animals,
having their bellies rubbed.

Some work only in goldleaf.
It is a painstaking labor.

Splashing the unnatural
unfolding of passion and greed

across a cryptic landscape.
Everything has been eaten.

The body of many brothers,
some an aggregate, a liquid

in disguise, like glass,
thermal and dramatic

a mystery that never explains
its halts and jerks

designing things seamless
and gilded. Some are advocates

of self preservation
and happiness, as if—why not?

# Excontemporary

What do people do in a town
close to Lake Erie on a Saturday morning
in August, crazy, crazy rock 'n' roll?
Silos and red wagons, corn
ripening in a tall stand—
we need so much—remembering

the dominant harmony when we fell
in love with the music, we said
what the music said first.
In our youth the chords
kept track of restlessness
as so many crossed
back and forth over its borders.

You were falling and falling
far away then but now
I've caught you smack
in the middle of the country,
the hotel laws of Ohio,

law of the road, rules of the game,
your recitation of an alphabet
you construct as you speak
outside the lane markers.

Not about anyone, the pillow fight,
the conversation at dinner,
passing small ponds,
green-lipped and unpopulated,
an idea of today.

Bunting personally centered above
the porch rail or as the come-on
for a used car dealer.

As if the last man encountered
the country for the first time.
From place to place, from time
to time, the upkeep on that particular
barn red, that wacky nationalism.

To continue to celebrate according
to his model for seizing year round
a confident rap on the door
from someone who knows he is welcome.

Once I thought I could know everything,
pink flowering grasses whose names
I do not know by the side of scant water
and clover, willows over
the wider water of Sandusky Bay.

An orchard, a campground, a marina,
spread across the lawn a long
cold style of house in contrast
to a cottage faced
with many small bright windows.

Can regret be dislodged
in imagining one of these other lives,
a woman kept as a souvenir
of his lost love
out in the middle of the lake

skittish about proximity to
the nuclear power plant?

Queen Anne's lace. You reach
over to my leg, just checking. Now
a field of plum-hued flowers
reaching almost all the way, almost clear
to as far as I can see.

# Biographical Note

Beth Baruch Joselow has been writing poems since she first learned to read. Her work includes eight books and chapbooks of poetry, with poems appearing in numerous magazines and anthologies, including *The New Yorker*, *The Washington Post*, *Boston Review*, and *American Poetry Review*.

During her years in Washington, D.C. she won four grants for poetry from the D.C. Commission on the Arts, and taught writing and liberal arts electives for 17 years as a member of the faculty at The Corcoran College of Art + Design. For several years she also served as literary editor for *The Washington Review of the Arts*.

She has written plays and non-fiction pieces for newspapers and magazines, art show catalogs, two non-fiction books on divorce, and *Writing Without the Muse*, a book of writing exercises. The *April Wars/The Fountains of Exhaustion*, an artists book made in an edition of 12 with Russian artist Pavel Makov, has been exhibited in galleries in the U.S. and Europe and is in the collection of the Osaka Museum in Japan.

Ms. Joselow now practices psychotherapy in Lewes, Delaware where she lives with her husband, poet Tom Mandel.

CPSIA information can be obtained
at www.ICGtesting.com
Printed in the USA
BVHW031750310321
603856BV00003B/36